Mexico Al Dia, 1948

Los Aguiluchos Por GUILLERMO JIMENEZ

Apolinar Navarrete and Hernan Traconis in *Mexico Al Dia*, 1948

Sing, Don't Cry

Angela Dominguez

Henry Holt and Company

New York

Henry Holt and Company
Publishers since 1866
175 Fifth Avenue, New York, New York 10010
mackids.com

Henry Holt® is a registered trademark of
Macmillan Publishing Group, LLC.
Copyright © 2017 by Angela Dominguez
All rights reserved.

Library of Congress Cataloging-in-Publication Data
Names: Dominguez, Angela.
Title: Sing, don't cry / Angela Dominguez.
Description: First edition. | New York : Henry Holt and Company, 2017.
Identifiers: LCCN 2016038378 | ISBN 9781627798396 (hardcover)
Subjects: LCSH: Diaz, Apolinar Navarrete de—Juvenile literature. | Musicians—Mexico—Biography—Juvenile literature.
Classification: LCC ML3930.D46 D6 2017 | DDC 781.62/68720092 [B]—dc23
LC record available at https://lccn.loc.gov/2016038378

Our books may be purchased in bulk for promotional, educational, or business use.
Please contact your local bookseller or the Macmillan Corporate and Premium Sales Department
at (800) 221-7945 ext. 5442 or by e-mail at MacmillanSpecialMarkets@macmillan.com.

First Edition—2017 / Designed by Liz Dresner
The illustrations for this book were created with pencil and tracing paper on Arches illustration board with digital color.
Printed in China by Toppan Leefung Printing Ltd., Dongguan City, Guangdong Province
1 3 5 7 9 10 8 6 4 2

Dedicated to my family,
especially my abuelo Apolinar

Once a year,
my abuelo would come
from Mexico to stay with us.

He always brought his guitar,

and he would sing to us every night.

He would tell us about his life,

and if we were sad about something,
he would say, "Sing, don't cry."

"Because singing
gladdens the heart."

When Abuelo was little, he had to
travel a long way to find a new home.

Just like us.

He told us singing made the distance seem smaller.

"Even when bad things happen,

you can still sing," Abuelo said.

"Some things may be lost forever,

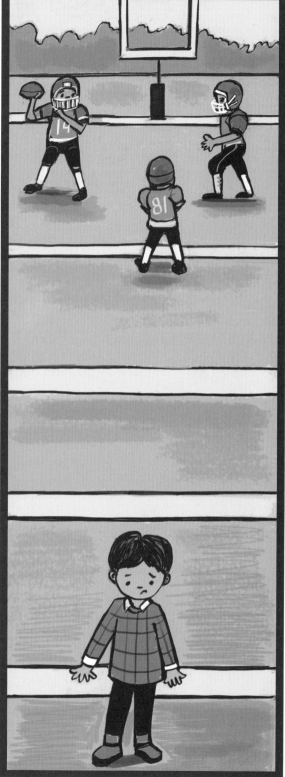

it's true."

"But maybe that makes room

for new and wonderful

things to be found."

"And eventually, you'll be able to walk tall."

"Sing, don't cry,

even when you are alone in a big city."

"Because singing can attract
someone to sing with you."

"When you are misunderstood,

and when people are unkind,

remember—sing, don't cry,

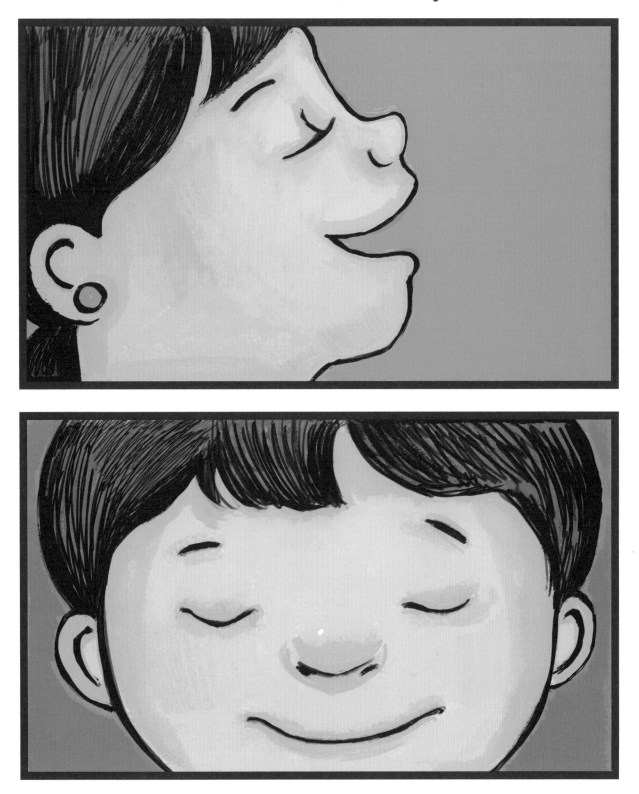

even if it is only in your soul."

"And always," Abuelo told us,
"I will be singing with you."

Author's Note

*Sing, Don't Cry is inspired by the refrain in
"Cielito lindo," a popular Mexican song.*

*Ay, ay, ay, ay,
canta y no llores,
porque cantando se alegran,
cielito lindo, los corazones.*

*Ay, ay, ay, ay,
sing and don't cry,
because singing gladdens
the heart, sweet lovely one.*

My grandfather Apolinar Navarrete Diaz was born in 1916. As a young boy, Apolinar and his family emigrated from the small town of Amealco, Querétaro, to Mexico City during the Mexican Revolution. When he lost his leg in a bus accident at the age of nine, he turned to music, learning the guitar. Apolinar grew up to be a musician, performing in a duo for an XEW radio show called *Los Aguiluchos*. Through it all, he was an extremely optimistic man who loved to share music and life with his loved ones. I carry that optimism and song in my heart. ♪

Los Aguiluchos—my abuelo Apolinar is on the left.

Me looking up fondly at Abuelo in Dallas, TX, 1984